The Hummer Garden

How to Increase Your Hummingbird Population

Laurel Rose Publishing

laurelrosepublishing@gmail.com

Dedication

My wife, Lisa has dedicated years to cultivating a unique backyard garden experience around her love of hummingbirds.

I can remember the days when we were excited to see even a couple of hummingbirds passing through on their annual migration.

Today, we start seeing these beautiful birds buzzing in our yard in late March and they are there in various numbers until late September.

Lisa's passion for these birds is astounding. During the peak time of the hummingbirds migration back to Mexico she is relentless in keeping her feeders filled each and every day to make sure that there is an ample supply of nectar.

This book is designed to share our hummingbird experience with anyone who also shares a passion for all God's creatures both great and small.

If you build the garden, they will come.

To my lovely wife and my best friend, Lisa Cockrell.

--Dr. Mike Cockrell

Writing a book isn't easy, any author and would be author will tell you so. But when it's a labor of love, as this book has been, then it's something you look forward to sitting down at your computer every day to do.

This book would not have been possible without the passion Lisa Cockrell has for hummingbirds and her love of nature. It wasn't until meeting her and Mike that I became drawn in to the wonderful and amazing world of Hummingbirds.

The pictures within this book are all a result of Lisa's love of experiencing the world through the lens of a camera.

As I write this dedication, Lisa has no idea this book is completed and about to be published. Her husband Mike and I thought it would be a wonderful gift for her birthday.

Happy Birthday Lisa, thanks for sharing you passion, love, and friendship with all of us.

--Chad R Martin

Table of Contents

Introduction

Hummingbirds are one of the most fascinating species of birds known to man; and also the least seen, except by those who know how to attract them. Most of us in America have seen a hummingbird at least once in our lives, yet they remain a mystery. When I first met the Cockrells I knew very little about hummingbirds outside of the fact that they flew very fast and I rarely ever saw one.

That all changed when I began visiting the Cockrell's home. It was summer and our local community theater, which I and their youngest daughter are a part of, were having our cast party at their wonderful home. Lisa Cockrell said she had something she wanted to show us.

When we walked out back to the pool area, I was amazed—there were hummingbirds everywhere! There were at least fifty hummingbirds! I told Lisa I had never seen anything like it. These birds were darting and hovering all around this beautiful patch of yard.

That's the day I learned about hummingbird gardens and how she had grown it and her hummingbird population to such a high number, creating a truly tranquil scene. It was over, I was a fan.

Fast forward three years later and Lisa now has well over a hundred hummingbirds visiting her garden every season. It is truly a wondrous and beautiful sight to behold. Since then she has had people from every walk of life ask her how she has managed it.

This book is a project of love, dedicated to helping other hummer lovers create beautiful and serene surroundings filled with one of nature's most amazing creature—the hummingbird.

Take this journey with us as Lisa Cockrell shares her beautiful pictures and inside knowledge on how she built her hummingbird garden and how you can build yours too!

A Message from Lisa

No matter if you have a large garden, or a small patio garden with containers, you can have a hummer garden to attract and enjoy hummingbirds. I have had both and have been enjoying Hummers for years. I keep my feeders up nearly year round. Taking them down when we have very cold weather that they might freeze.

They start their migration north early spring and migrate back in early fall. I have had the pleasure of having my first in early March, and my very last one in late November. Having feeders out will not make them delay their migration, but you certainly can help that straggler that is sometimes migrating through late.

"Good things come to those who wait... Better things come to those who don't give up...and the best things come to those who believe!
"

If you hang even one feeder, and plant even one plant, then I believe they will come. These beautiful birds tend to follow their same migration pattern and be assured that if they find your place early or late, they will be back. They will be back to raise their young and invite their friends. I very much feel it is a blessing to enjoy these beautiful birds and to share their beauty with others.

I hope you enjoy The Hummer Garden, and wish you the best in building your own. The beauty and love are yours to share and treasure for many years to come.

Creating Your Garden

Trees

"There is always music amongst the trees in the Garden, but our hearts must be very quiet to hear it."
— Minnie Aumonier

Most How-to books start by giving you a history of whatever subject it is you are wishing to learn about and generally you don't get down to the brass tacks until at least half-way through the book. Well, we are going to dive right in! This is why you bought this book after all!

The best place to start your hummingbird project is with the actual foliage itself. You are going to want to build your hummer garden where there is a combination of sun and shade, so pick a nice spot that is relevant to your needs. This can be as small or as large as you want, some take up several acres.

Avoid the pitfalls of not planning out how to best build your hummingbird garden. Too many times people just throw any old plants together and expect instant overwhelming results. Now, it doesn't have to be an artistic sketch but rather something that gives you a vision and help keeps that vision on track.

Build yours to suit your surroundings. The whole point of building one, after all, is to enjoy the sight of these beautiful creatures. So pick a style that allows our winged friends to dart around in the sun but also offers a spot for them to cool off and nest their young.

At the end of this book we will have a list of hummingbird friendly foliage.

Here is how Lisa built her hummer garden:

"I have azaleas, chaste tree, butterfly bush, magnolia trees, and wax myrtles that are for coverage and color. The vine I have is called a cross vine. The chaste trees are the best! The hummers drink the nectar from the blooms and take cover. Plus, these are plants that stay. You don't have to plant every year!"

This is the foundation for a beautiful and effective garden. You can also use Eucalyptus or Bottlebrush trees because of the soft materials that the hummingbirds can use to build their nests. Crabapple trees and the English Hawthorn tree are also great hummingbird attractant trees.

Willow trees are also an excellent choice as it gives the hummers a sturdy, shaded place to build their nests.

And to touch on nests for a moment, try to build vertical with trellises as well, allowing vines to grow upwards. Moss and lichen are also great to have as hummingbirds love to build nests out of the soft foliage.

Here are a few suggestions for trees and vines.

Trees and Shrubs

- **Azalea** – Flowers in early spring and late summer and produces bright red-orange flowers.
- **Butterfly Bush (Buddleia)** - Purple, orange and a whitish color blooms that can grow to be ten inches tall.
- **Cape Honeysuckle** – Although not a traditional honeysuckle, this tropical plant grows best in full sunlight.
- **Chaste Tree** – A small ornamental tree that more often than not has small clusters of lilac flowers. (Lisa's trees are 12-15 ft tall!)

- **Flame Acanthus** – A heat loving small shrub the blooms with red and orange blossoms from midsummer to frost.
- **Flowering Quince** – A member of the rose family, this shrub has spiny branches with usually red or pink flowers.
- **Lantana** – Cultivated for their bright and aromatic yellow and orange flowers, this widely introduced shrub has dense spikes or umbels.
- **Magnolia** – A beautiful flowering tree that produces pink, purple, or yellowish flowers.
- **Manzanita** – This is a small evergreen shrub that produces white or pink flowers in drooping panicles.
- **Mimosa** – A fast growing tree with yellow flowers (Lisa's are pink, depends on location), dripping with nectar that hummingbirds love.
- **Red Buckeye** – A favorite of the red-throated hummingbird, it's tubular, carmine red bloom, is full of nectar.

- **Tree Tobacco** – It's a fast growing, frost sensitive plant with clusters of yellow blossoms on the tips of its branches.
- **Turk's Cap** – A low maintenance, tough, woody shrub, whose flowers look like small red turbans.
- **Wax Myrtles** – An evergreen shrub that has small berry-like fruit with a waxy coating.
- **Weigela** – An Asian shrub that has clusters of pink, purple, red, or white showy bell-shaped flowers.

Vines – support with a trellis

- **Coral Honeysuckle** - The vine is evergreen with beautiful orange-red tubular flowers that bloom in clusters.
- **Cypress Vine** – It grows as an annual vine with small red blooms that once established doesn't require much attention.
- **Morning Glory** – Another tubular shape, gorgeous vine that is easy to grow and hummingbirds love.
- **Scarlet Runner Bean** – A very fast growing annual vine that produces very attractive and edible bright red flowers.
- **Snapdragon** – A smaller vine that can be potter or hung from porches and decks with glossy, ivy-shaped leaves and tubular flowers that attract hummers and butterflies.
- **Trumpet Creeper** – With 3 to 4 inch orange, red, or yellow flowers shaped like the bell of a trumpet, it is a long blooming source of food for hummers.

Flowers

"Gardens and flowers have a way of bringing people together, drawing them from their homes."
— Clare Ansberry

Flowers are an integral part of every hummingbird garden. While hummingbirds don't have a great sense of smell (practically none) they DO have incredible eyesight which makes them very visual creatures. Hummingbirds love the color red as well as other bright, inviting colors. This makes beautiful, welcoming flowers a must for every hummingbird garden.

When Lisa was choosing flowers for her hummingbird garden, it was very important to her to have the right types of flowers.

"I wanted flowers that had the colors and textures to attract hummingbirds and butterflies. What we decided on were Moon Flowers, Gardenias, Petunias, Day Lilies, Roses, and Gladiolas. The hummingbirds love the bright colors, and so do we."

Hummingbirds love tubular flowers; the trumpet vine is a great example of this. But try to avoid hybrid flowers as they don't produce as much nectar as wild flowers do. Hummingbirds will naturally pollinate your flowers which helps keep a beautiful, blossoming garden.

Colorful varieties will keep your amazing little visitors coming back for more. Just as humans don't like to eat the same exact things over and over, neither do hummingbirds. Don't hesitate to be creative.

Hummingbirds cross the 500 mile stretch of the Gulf of Mexico in an 18-20 hours period of non-stop flight! Imagine how much energy they expend and how much they need to refuel their little engines.

A beautiful, garden with inviting flowers full of delicious nectar is just the thing these incredible birds need after such an arduous journey.

Hummers also help to pollinate your garden as they move from flower to flower, spreading the pollen and helping to keep the garden constantly growing and flourishing.

Lisa's hummingbird garden also double's as a meditation garden. It's perfect for relaxation and enjoying the beauty of what nature has to offer.

Here is a list of flowers that Hummingbirds love. We took this list directly from dianeseeds.com as it is a very good directory for giving you many possible ideas on how to fill your garden to once again suit your style while pleasing the hummers with flowers and nectars that they love! We also threw in a few of our own highlighted in bold blue. Use these as a starting point for your beautiful hummer garden.

It is important to note that many of these flowers only grow to their best in certain zones so it is equally imperative to be sure of the zone you live in. The map that follows this list will give you a reference point as to the zone you live in.

- **Agastache rupestris** (Sunset Hyssop) – Also called Licorice Mint it is a hummingbird favorite with orange-coral and pink petalled & lavender-calyxed flower spikes, it can last from mid-summer to mid-autumn.

- **Asclepias tuberosa** (Butterfly Weed) – A North American milkweed with bright orange flowers.
- **Aquilegia** (Columbine) – A perennial herb with various colored flowers that have petals and long hollow flowers.
- **Cleome** – With white or purplish flowers and long stamens, this plant is also called the spider flower.
- **Cosmos 'Ladybird Scarlet'** – A scarlet-orange colored flower that bloom on compact plants during mid-summer.
- Day Lilies - This plant has grass-like leaves and large yellow, orange, or red lily-like flowers, which typically last for only one day but are quickly replaced by others.
- **Digitalis** (Foxglove) – Although poisonous to animals this beautiful purple bulb is a favorite of hummingbirds.
- **Eupatorium** (Joe-Pye Weed) – This tall composite weed has clusters of pinkish or purple flowers.
- **Gaura** – This plant has a bloom shaped like a lance that comes in pink, cream, or gold depending on the variety.
- Gardenias – These beautiful shrubs have glossy evergreen leaves that have large, fragrant, white flowers.
- Gladiolas – Sometimes called the "Sword Lily" this bulbous flower come in a variety of colors from pink to reddish or light purple with white, contrasting markings, or white to cream or orange to red.
- **Goldenrod** – A composite plant that has numerous vivid yellow flower heads.
- **Hesperis matronalis** – A native of the mustard family, this is a four petal flower that comes in beautiful shades of purple and lavender.
- **Hibiscus** – This flower, known for its large conspicuous blooms comes in a variety of attractant colors: red, orange, white, pink, purple, and yellow.
- **Impatiens balsamina** (Garden Blossom) – An annual plant whose leaves are arranged spirally, blooms in either red, pink, purple, or white.
- **Ipomoea** (Morning Glory) – Have funnel shaped flowers that close late in the day.

- **Ipomopsis rubra** (Standing Cypress) – A sparsely leaved biennial with showy red tubular flowers.
- **Liatris** – This plant has spikes of long purplish flowers.
- **Lobelia cardinalis** – A North American lobelia that has brilliant red flowers
- **Lupine** - A plant that belongs to the legume family. It's flowers are tall dense clusters of blue, pink, or white.
- **Lychnis chalcedonica** (Maltese Cross) – Popular in cottage gardens, these flowers are produced in clusters and are bright red.
- **Mirabilis jalapa** (Four O'Clock) – A beautiful plant with an unusual aspect, it's flowers change colors over time. Hummers love this trumpet shaped flower.
- Moon Flowers – Related to morning glories, this plant is best known for its night blooming white flowers.
- **Monarda** (Bee Balm) – A member of the mint family, these small, bright red flowers are a favorite of both hummingbirds and butterflies.
- **Nicotiana** (Flowering Tobacco) – A star shaped member of the tobacco family, this flower is sure to liven up any garden with its multitude of colors.
- **Penstemon** (Beardtongue) – There are many varieties of beardtongue, with brilliantly colored tubular flowers.
- **Perovskia atriplicifolia** (Russian Sage) – A great highlight to any garden with its lavender-blue colored flowers.
- **Petunia** – A funnel shaped flower known for its colors of white, pink, blue, or puple.
- Roses – While not a nectar producer, hummers tend to drink the water that has collected there after rainstorms and also little insects.
- **Salvia** (Sage) – Native of California, hummers love this magenta colored flower.
- **Scarlet runner bean** - A very fast growing annual vine that produces very attractive and edible bright red flowers.
- **Silene 'Jack Flash'** – A beautiful plant with orangey-red starburst blooms.

- **Sweet pea** – A member of the pea family with pastel colored butterfly shaped flowers.
- **Tithonia 'Torch'** - Another tall composite plant with yellow or orange-red ray flowers.
- **Verbena bonariensis** – A perennial that has clusters of rich lilac cluster flowers.
- **Zinnia** - This plant has a solitary head with brightly colored flowers.

There are many top 10 lists out there for which plants best attract hummingbirds. And while they vary in several ways, here are the top 5 that most agree on.

Top 5 Hummingbird Attractive Plants:

1. Bee Balm
2. Cardinal Flower
3. Trumpet Creeper
4. Columbine
5. Fuchsia

Honorable Mentions: Zinnia, Salvia, Hollyhock, Petunia, Butterfly Bush, Bleeding Heart

There are many more flowers you can use, especially depending on the zone you are in. You can research these as well as an even bigger list in John Lively's book: Hummingbirds and Flowers They Love

Abelia, azalea, begonia, bleeding heart, bovardia, butterfly bush, canna lily, catmint, chelone, clematis, crabapple, crocosmia, dahlia, Dicliptera suberecta, flowering quince, fuchsia, geranium, gladiolus, hawthorne, heuchera, hosta, honeysuckle, iris, kniphofia, lantana, lilac, lily, mock orange, nasturtium, pentas, phlox, physostegia, rose of sharon, Stachys coccinea, trumpet vine, veronica, weigela, wisteria, yucca, zauschneria.

Average Annual Minimum Temperature

Temperature (°F)	Zone Color	Temperature (°C)
Below -50.0	1 Goldenrod	-45.6 and below
< -40 to -50	2 Cornflower	< -40.0 to -45.5
< -30 to -40	3 Carrot	< -34.5 to -40.0
< -20 to -30	4 Violet	< -28.9 to -34.4
< -10 to -20	5 Apple	< -23.4 to -28.8
< 0 to -10	6 Buttercup	< -17.8 to -23.3
< 10 to 0	7 Rose	< -12.3 to -17.7
< 20 to 10	8 Moss	< -6.7 to -12.2
< 30 to 20	9 Peach	< -1.2 to -6.6
< 40 to 30	10 Poinsettia	< 4.4 to -1.1
< 50 to 40	11 Peppermint	< 10.0 to 4.5
< 60 to 50	12 Melon	< 15.5 to 10.0
< 70 to 60	13 Bluebell	< 21.1 to 15.6
< 80 to 70	14 Orchid	< 26.6 to 21.2
80 and above	15 Papaya	26.7 and above

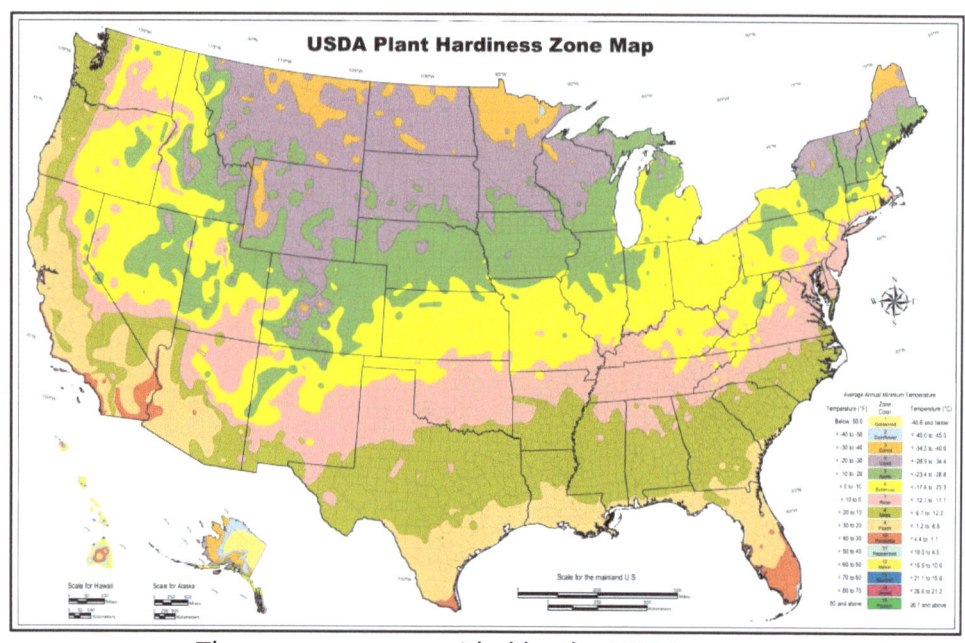

These maps are provided by the USDA

Remember, there are enough flowers, trees, shrubs and vines out there for you to create a unique beautiful garden that will attract these amazing aerial visitors and keep them coming back year after year.

Feeders

A flash of harmless lightning, A mist of rainbow dyes, The burnished sunbeams brightening, From flower to flower he flies

--John Banister Tabb

Okay, your garden is about done. You have all these wonderful plants and trees, possibly even stone benches to sit and view this wonder, but there is still one thing missing--feeders.

Feeders are a very important element to any hummingbird garden. Are they mandatory for a hummer's survival?

Obviously not.

But what it does do is give a surplus of nectar for these energetic birds that can be far easier to get to than nectar from flowers. That doesn't mean you shouldn't have natural flowers and trees; it simply means that interspersing your garden with fresh filled feeders can help to draw in more hummers and keep them coming back from season to season.

The thing to know about hummingbird feeders is that there are a huge variety to choose from. However, not all feeders are created equal. Choosing the appropriate feeder for your garden can mean the difference between a few stragglers or multitude of these aerodynamic wonders.

The following are the types of feeders that Lisa has used to great success in her hummer garden. Again, that doesn't mean you are limited to these, it's just what she has had the most success with. Lisa also prefers glass to plastic, as glass doesn't mildew the way plastic does.

A version of the Four Fountains Feeder, this feeder is very popular and easy to fill.

The HummZinger© feeder, as shown above, is a very good feeder, especially if you have bee and wasp problems. While it doesn't hold very much nectar it IS very easy to clean.

This is another great feeder that hummers love!

There are many novelty feeders to choose from but in our experience, to have the most success, there are a select few that you should include in your garden.

Below is a list of the top four feeders as compiled by Gardenexperiments.com and a link to purchase them if you don't have access to a store around you that sells them.

- HummZinger Excel
- Best-1 Hummingbird Feeder
- Four Flower Frolic Hummingbird Feeder

- [Dr. JB's Clean Hummingbird Feeder](#)

http://astore.amazon.com/laurrosepubl-20   This link has all of the feeders and cleaning tools that Lisa uses in her hummer garden.

Insects

"One of the problems with having a garden that attracts Hummingbirds is that it will attract bees and wasps. Even though Honey Bees and bumblebees are good for the environment, they are not always welcome visitors around my feeders."

Insects, especially wasps, yellow jackets, hornets and bees, can be an unwanted and dangerous nuisance to not only the hummingbirds but yourself as well. You want your hummers to be able to fly and eat freely without the hassle of bees putting a damper on their exploits.

Wasp, yellow jackets, and hornets are very aggressive and will constantly attack the hummers until they drive them away so they can feed on the nectar themselves.

Not all insects are bad. In fact, hummers need to eat bugs for protein to help fuel the enormous amounts of energy they burn. Hummingbirds also help keep the gnat population under control.

Here are a few tips for holding them at bay:

"I do avoid commercial pesticides because of the harm to other insects and the hummingbirds themselves, but I do a few tricks to keep them off my feeders. One such trick is a wasp catcher. These are beautiful addition to the garden, and they serve several purposes.

They help to eliminate wasps and flies without exposing your family or your yard to toxic chemicals. Bees will get in them as well but they are somewhat smarter creatures and tend to see dead insects and will just leave the area.

First, hang the wasp catchers on a Sheppard's hook or other decorative stand and fill with sugar water or lemonade to entice wasps and other stinging insects. They will fly in the hole in the bottom, but are not able to climb out and they will die. Make sure to clean this out often and no one will ever know your new decorative accessory to your hummer garden is even used for pest control."

Dangers

"And I say also this. I do not think the forest would be so bright, nor the water so warm, nor love so sweet, if there were no danger in the lakes."
— *C.S. Lewis, Out of the Silent Planet*

In all the wilds there are dangers all about. It is no different for hummingbirds. As majestic as these birds are, and as with any species, there are always things that threaten them. Some of these dangers are natural while others are manmade.

"Hummingbirds can be trapped inside garages and buildings. They will die if not removed quickly. Be aware of hummers in garages especially because they are attracted to the red emergency cords. Keep garage doors closed and check the area carefully after they have been opened."

Predators, as one would imagine, are a huge danger for hummers. Squirrels, chipmunks, crows, blue jays, are all a serious threat to our zippy little friends. Even snakes, fish, and frogs have been known to snatch some of our low flying friends.

But of all the dangers from other animals, varmints, or insects, cats seem to pose the biggest threat. Cats love to chase and pounce after hummingbirds.

Weather is also a big threat to hummingbirds, especially during the migration periods. Storms over the Gulf of Mexico have been known to force the birds into the water, causing them to drown.

While it doesn't happen as much, man-made hazards have claimed the lives of more than a few hummers. As intuitive as these birds are they have been known to fly into windows and mirrors. Sometimes all it takes is to move a long-standing object to another place other than what the bird is used to.

There is no way to prevent all of these dangers from coming about, however, be mindful of the environment you create your hummer garden in so as to minimize the potential of danger.

Nectar

Work without Hope draws nectar in a sieve,
And Hope without an object cannot live.

-    *Samuel Taylor Coleridge*

As we near the completion of this labor of love we thought we would leave you with some of the easy and best nectar recipes for your hummers to enjoy. Some of you may wish to buy your nectar from a store. For those who don't, simply follow the steps below.

A few cautions:

DON'TS

- Don't use honey, brown sugar or molasses.

- If your water contains heavy chemicals consider using purified water.
- Don't use sugar substitutes. They need the calories for energy.
- Don't fill feeders until nectar is completely cool, otherwise it will ferment quicker.

There are also a few preventative measures that you can take to ensure your feeders are in the best condition to hold the nectar you are feeding to the hummingbirds.

Preventative Measures:

- Nectar can be stored in a refrigerator for up to a week.
- Additives are not essential for a hummingbird's health. A simple sugar mixture is all they require.
- Clean feeders at least once a week and replenish with fresh nectar.

Some of you may be wondering about the red dye in the nectar. While it is not necessary to add it to the mixture, a lot of people do as it is non-toxic.

The red color of the nectar doesn't add as an attractant for the hummers but it does seem to blur the view of hummingbirds who may be feeding on the other side of the feeder. As hummers aren't very social creatures, this can help lessen the aggression of battling over nectar.

So, the choice is yours. Personally, we love the red color.

Lisa's Recipe

- 1 cup of Pure Cane White Granulated Sugar
- 4 cups of cold water

"I've stopped using commercial products. If you have trouble attracting birds use red surveyor's tape. Replace mixture when it becomes cloudy. Hot weather spoils the nectar."

Lisa sometimes mixes her nectar cold and sometimes she boils the water, adds the sugar and nectar powder, stirring well, and allows the mixture to completely cool before pouring into the feeders.

Traditional Recipe

- 1 cup Pure Cane White Granulated Sugar.
- 4 cups hot boiling water

Boil more than four (4) cups of water on the stove top. When you use more than four (4) cups of water, you can adjust to the loss of water from steam. Carefully measure out four (4) cups of boiling water into a large bowl. Add one (1) cup of pure cane white granulated sugar. Mix the pure cane white granulated sugar and water together until all of the sugar is dissolved. Carefully place the mixture into the refrigerator to cool, usually overnight. When mixture is cold, take the mixture out of the refrigerator. You now have a bowl of hummingbird food.

We hope you found this book informative and helpful in the creation of your own hummingbird garden. These birds are beautiful to look at and a thrill to behold. They are also an amazing study of nature's wonder.

The steps outlined in this book are what helped Lisa grow her hummingbird population to the staggering amount it is today (over 100 hummers at any given time) and that number continues to grow annually.

We would love to hear from you.

Send us your success stories and pictures at https://www.facebook.com/hummergarden

Hummingbird Species

"A flash of harmless lightning, A mist of rainbow dyes, The burnished sunbeams brightening, From flower to flower he flies."

-John Banister Tabb

When we think of hummingbirds when think of these fast little zippy fliers. But what most people don't realize is that the hummingbird is a vast and varied species.

Did you know that there are over 350 different types of hummingbirds? That's an amazing number! Many of them are on the endangered species list.

While many of these species live in Central and South America there are a few that call North America home: Allen's, Anna's, Costa's, Ruby-Throated, and Rufous. We won't go into great detail but here are a few facts for each of these North American favorites.

Allen's: Found mostly in California and lower Oregon, the Allen's can be identified by it's green back and forehead, with rust-colored rufous flanks, rump, and tail. The male has an iridescent orange-red throat while the females and immatures have speckled throats.

Anna's: Named after Anna Massena, Duchess of Rivoli, it has a bronze-green back, a pale grey chest and belly, and green flanks. The male has an iridescent crimson-red crown and throat, and a dark, slightly forked tail. It is the only North American hummingbird species with a red crown. They are found along the western coast of North America, from southern Canada to northern Baja California, and inland to southern Arizona; although some have been spotted in New York and Florida.

Costa's: A very small hummingbird, the male Costa's has a mainly green back and flanks, a small black tail and wings, and patches of white below their gorgeted throat and tail. The male Costa's Hummingbird's most distinguishing feature is its vibrant purple cap and throat with the throat feathers flaring out and back behind its head. This common hummer can be found from the Southwestern United States to the Baja California Peninsula of Mexico.

Ruby-Throated: This small animal is the only species of hummingbird that regularly nests east of the Mississippi River in North America(You will see many of these in Lisa's pics). Adults are metallic green above and greyish white below, with near-black wings. The adult male, has a ruby red throat patch.

Rufous: This beautiful bird has a white breast, rufous face, upper parts, flanks and tail and an iridescent orange-red throat patch (gorget). Some males have some green on back and/or crown. The female has green upper parts with some white, some iridescent orange feathers in the center of the throat, and a dark tail with white tips and rufous base. Their breeding habitat is open areas and forest edges in western North America from southern Alaska to California.

Sources

We would like to think Homestead Farms in Coldwater, Mississippi for helping bring our Hummer Garden to life.

When writing a book it is necessary to do lots of research to make sure your facts are as accurate as possible. Below is a list of incredible resources we used to help flesh out our book.

We invite you to visit these wonderful sites to learn even more about hummingbirds, the environments they live in, and the incredible journeys they take.

- Dianeseeds.com
- Aggie-horticulture.tamu.edu
- Thedailysouth.southernliving.com
- Hummingbirds.net
- Thefreedictionary.com
- Fireflyforest.com
- Houstonaudobon.org
- Hummingbird-guide.com
- Worldofhummingbirds.com
- En.wikipedia.org
- Gardenexperiments.com

www.ingramcontent.com/pod-product-compliance
Lightning Source LLC
Chambersburg PA
CBHW050842290526
45792CB00001B/494